I0751811

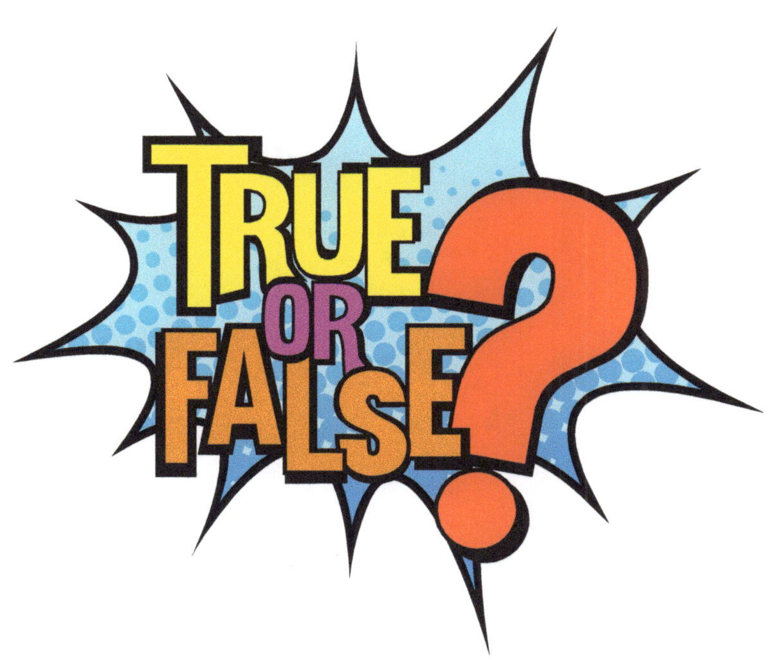
TRUE
OR
FALSE?

Co-published by agreement between Shi Tu Hui and World Book, Inc.

Shi Tu Hui
Room 1807, Block 1,
#3 West Dawang Road
Chaoyang District, Beijing 100025
P.R. China

World Book, Inc.
180 North LaSalle Street
Suite 900
Chicago, Illinois 60601
USA

Copyright © 2024. All rights reserved. This volume may not be reproduced in whole or in part in any form without prior written permission from the publishers.

WORLD BOOK and the GLOBE DEVICE are registered trademarks or trademarks of World Book, Inc.

Library of Congress Cataloging-in-Publication Data for this volume has been applied for.

True or False? (set #4)
ISBN: 978-0-7166-5417-9 (set, hc.)

Civil Rights
ISBN: 978-0-7166-5421-6 (hc.)

Also available as:
ISBN: 978-0-7166-5431-5 (e-book)
ISBN: 978-0-7166-5441-4 (soft cover)

Staff

Executive Committee

President
Geoff Broderick

Vice President, Editorial
Tom Evans

Vice President, Finance
Molly Stedron

Vice President, International and Marketing
Eddy Kisman

Vice President, Technology and Operations
Jason Dole

Director, Human Resources
Bev Ecker

Editorial

Writer
Jeff De La Rosa

Manager, New Content
Jeff De La Rosa

Associate Manager, New Content
William D. Adams

Curriculum Designer
Caroline Davidson

Proofreader
Nathalie Strassheim

Graphics and Design

Coordinator, Design Development & Production:
Brenda Tropinski

Senior Visual Communications Designer
Melanie Bender

Senior Media Editor
Rosalia Bledsoe

TRUE OR FALSE?

CIVIL RIGHTS

WORLD BOOK
www.worldbook.com

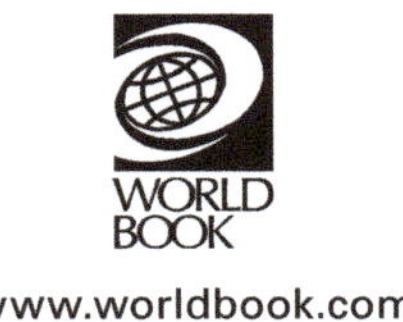

CIVIL RIGHTS

TRUE OR FALSE?

Civil rights include freedom of speech, freedom of the press, and freedom of religion.

TRUE!

They also include the right to own property and to be treated fairly by the government and others.

FOR
SALE

8

TRUE OR FALSE?

Freedom of speech gives you the right to say anything you want.

Freedom of speech does not protect speech that leads to unnecessary harm. For example, it does not protect a person who causes a panic by falsely shouting "FIRE!" in a crowded public building.

TRUE OR FALSE?

In the United States, the president and Congress generally have the final say on civil rights issues.

13

FALSE!

The courts—especially the Supreme Court—have probably done the most to define civil rights.

LAW

TRUE OR FALSE?

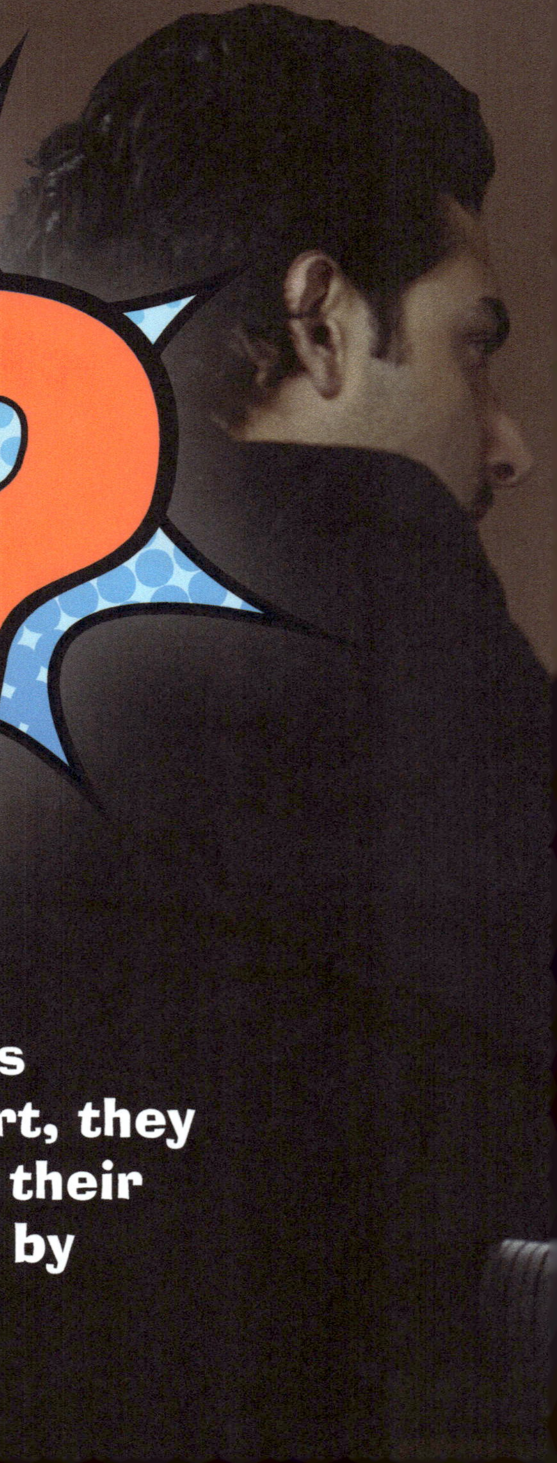

When defendants "take the fifth" in court, they are pleading to have their sentence reduced by one-fifth.

FALSE!

A defendant who "takes the fifth" is invoking the Fifth Amendment to the U.S. Constitution. It protects people from being forced to testify against themselves.

TRUE OR FALSE?

Modern democracies have generally been eager to acknowledge the rights of minorities.

21

STOP
HATE & VIOLENCE

FALSE!

Many minorities have struggled to achieve recognition of their civil rights through protests, court decisions, and other work. These struggles continue today.

TRUE OR FALSE?

During World War II (1939-1945), the United States imprisoned more than 100,000 people of Japanese ancestry in camps out of fear they might aid Japan.

TRUE!

Most of those imprisoned under the policy, called *internment,* were U.S. citizens. The Civil Liberties Act of 1988 granted survivors an apology for violating their civil rights.

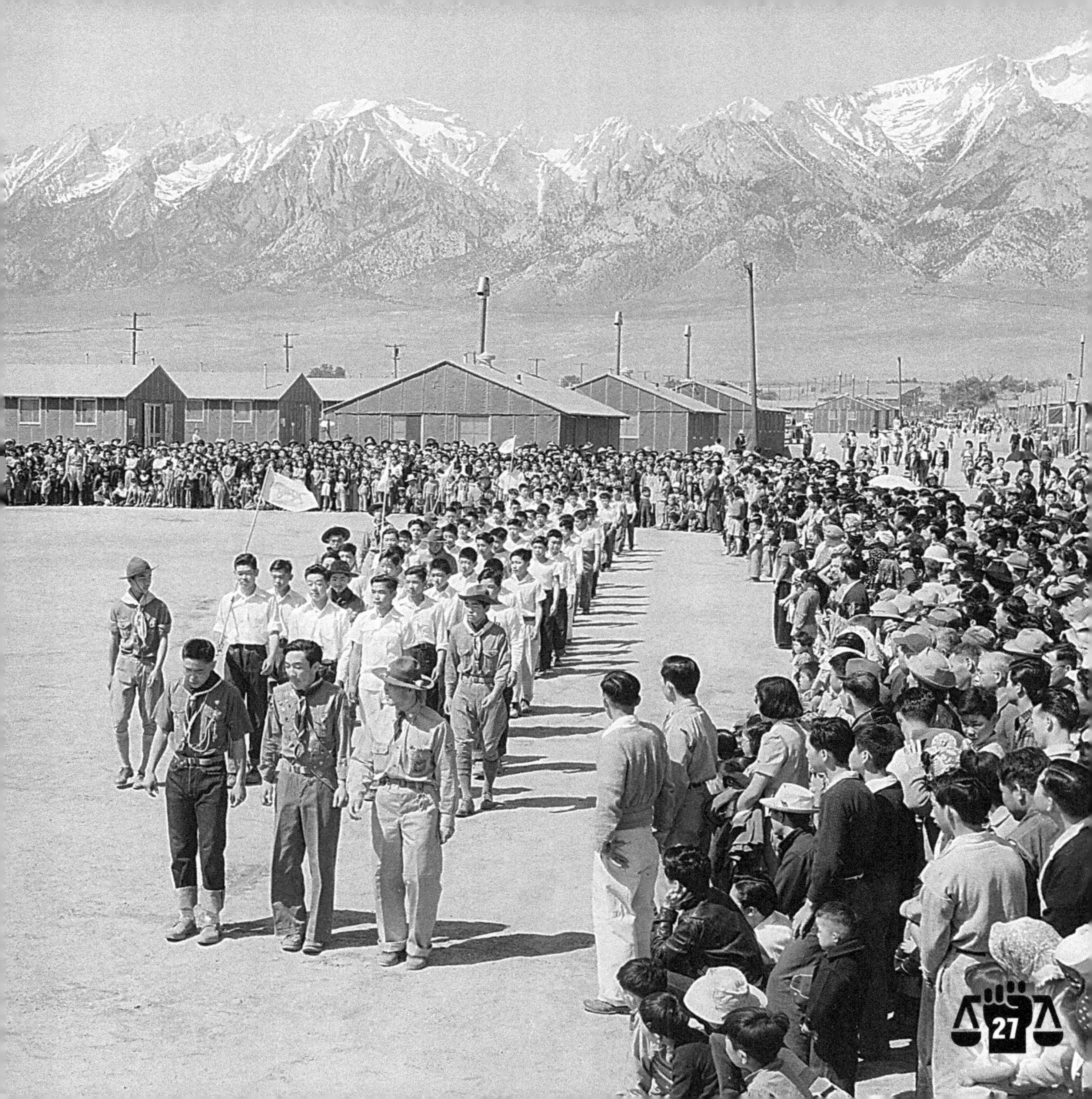

TRUE OR FALSE?

Poll taxes were once charged to help fund elections.

PAY
POLL TAX
HERE

FALSE!

Poll taxes were charged to prevent the poor, often formerly enslaved Black people, from voting. In 1966, the U.S. Supreme Court ruled this practice illegal.

VOTE

VOTE

VOTE
STOP BRUTALITY in ALABAMA
Negroes Are Americans Too Protect Them
Negroes Are Americans Too
We Demand THE RIGHT TO VOTE EVERY-WHERE
STOP BRUTALITY in ALABAMA
We Demand THE RIGHT TO VOTE EVERY-WHERE
THE MINISTERS URGE THE PRESIDENT TO ACCEPT MORAL RESPONSIBILITY
TE

POLICE

TRUE OR FALSE?

During the Stonewall uprising, the police laid siege to protesters sheltering behind stone walls.

FALSE!

The Stonewall uprising was a series of demonstrations for gay rights that took place in New York City in 1969. The uprising began when police raided a bar called the Stonewall Inn.

The Stonewall Inn
STOP THE HATE
LOVE CONQUERS HATE
#orlando
JUNE 12th 2016
SAY THEIR NAMES
DAD TO MY SON
Love You More
NYC
MARSHA P. JOHNSON
We are Orlando

TRUE
OR
FALSE?

A group of *Indigenous* (native) protesters once occupied the famous prison island of Alcatraz.

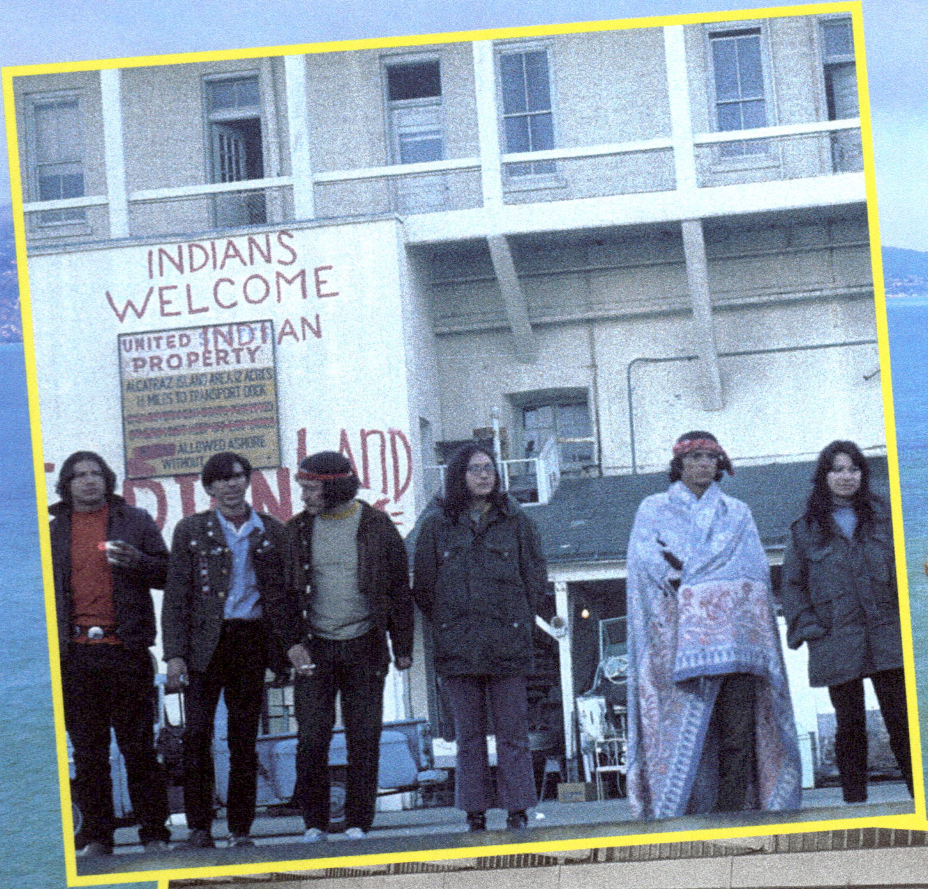
INDIANS
WELCOME
INDIAN
PROPERTY
LAND

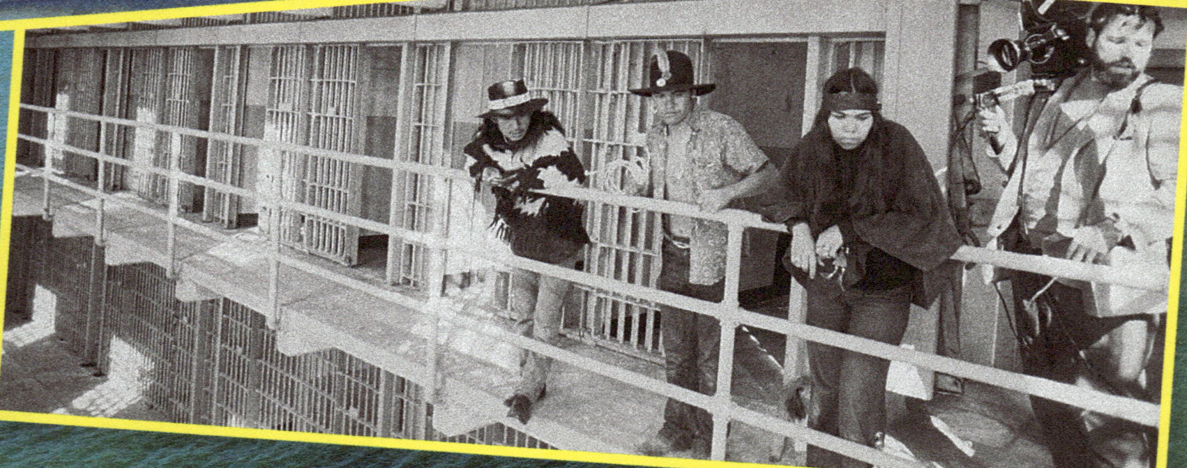

The prison, located in San Francisco Bay, closed in 1963. Protesters occupied the island from 1969 to 1971. They sought to bring attention to Indigenous land claims and civil rights.

POLICE

TRUE OR FALSE?

A person's Miranda rights, often read upon arrest, include the right to remain silent and the right to an attorney.

TRUE!

The name comes from the Supreme Court decision in the case of *Miranda v. Arizona.* In that case, Ernesto A. Miranda complained that he had given a confession without knowing his rights.

200
100
1
2

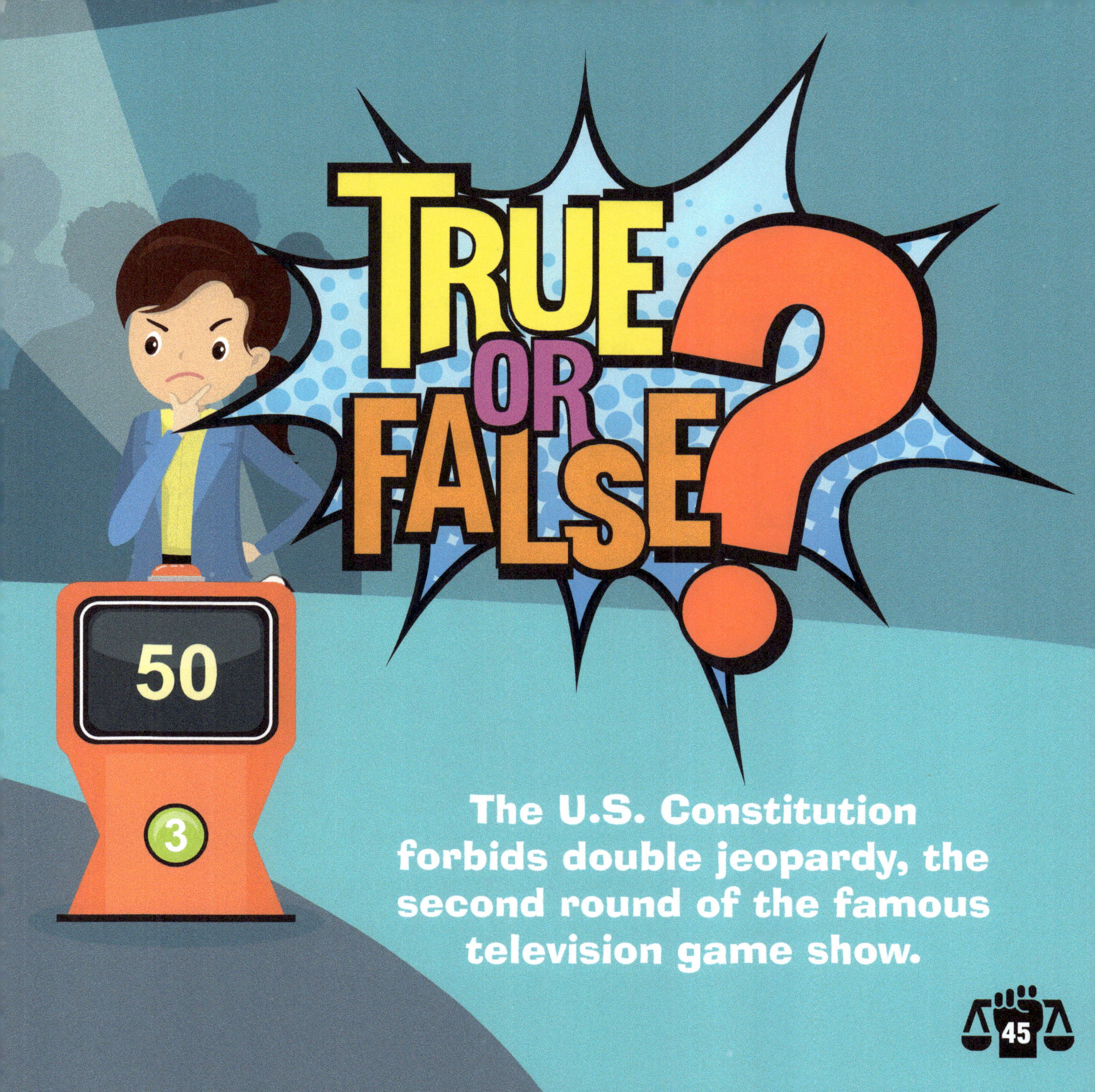

The U.S. Constitution forbids double jeopardy, the second round of the famous television game show.

FALSE!

The *double jeopardy* forbidden by the Constitution means *trying a person twice for the same crime.*

TRUE OR FALSE?

Even kings are not entirely above the law.

TRUE!

The Magna Carta, signed in 1215, outlined the limits of the king of England's power and his duty to some of his subjects. The signing of this document is one of the most important events in the history of democracy.

TRUE
OR
FALSE?

Though the Declaration of Independence reads "all men are created equal," this was widely understood to include women at the time.

FALSE!

Our modern understanding of the Declaration generally extends to all people. But at the time, its protections excluded women, Blacks, Indigenous people, and others.

55

TRUE OR FALSE?

The White House was built in part using enslaved labor.

Enslaved people were involved in many stages of construction, from the quarrying and transportation of stone to the building of the White House. They worked alongside European artisans, white laborers, and other free African American wage laborers.

TRUE OR FALSE?

Black students were welcomed into integrated schools after *segregation* (separation of the races) was ruled illegal.

FALSE!

Many people continued to oppose the integration of schools. The 6-year-old Ruby Bridges, one of the first Black children to integrate an elementary school in the Deep South, had to be escorted to class past angry mobs.

64

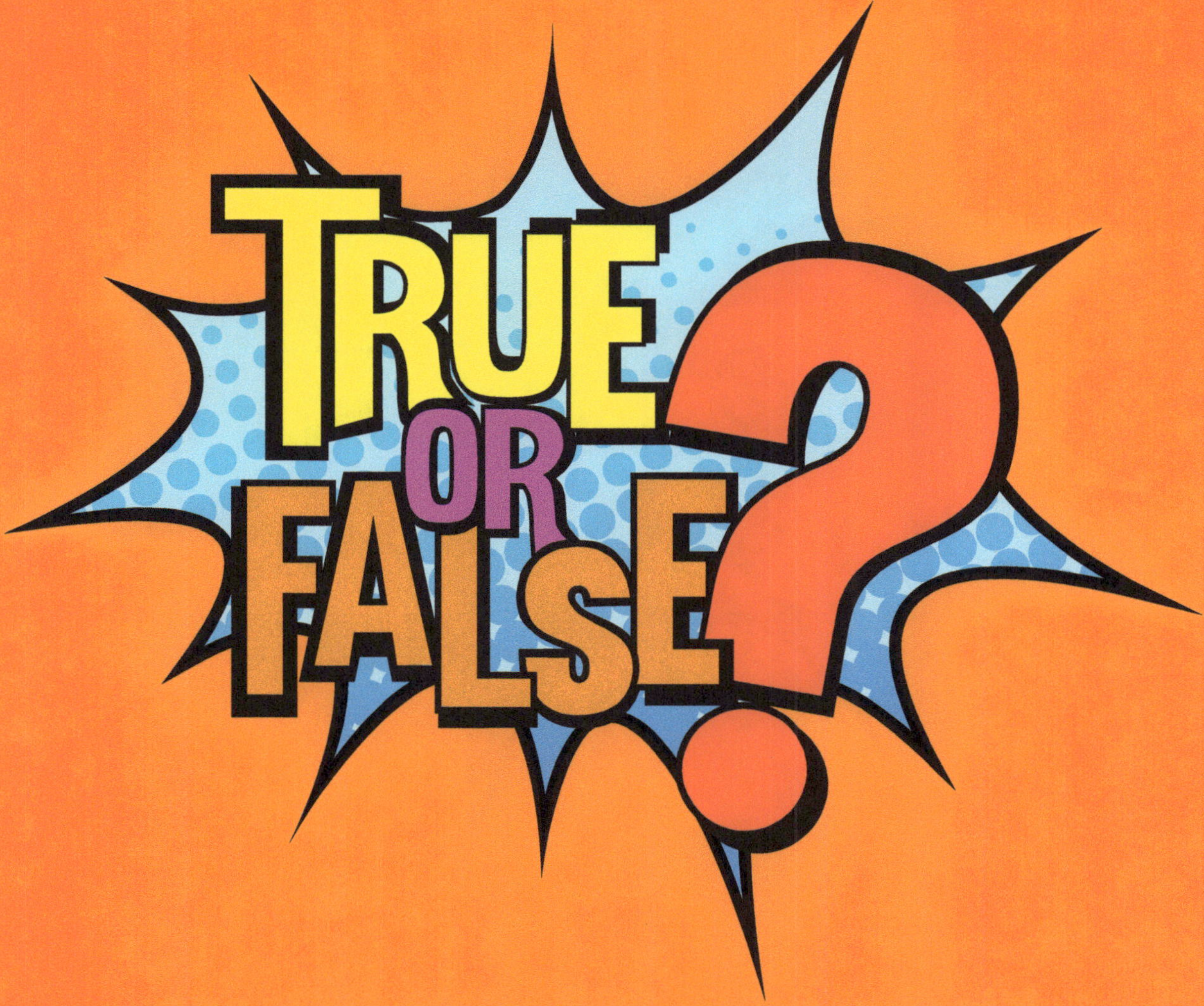

TRUE OR FALSE?

The civil rights leader Martin Luther King, Jr., won a Nobel Peace Prize.

TRUE!

King won the 1964 Nobel Peace Prize for leading nonviolent civil rights demonstrations.

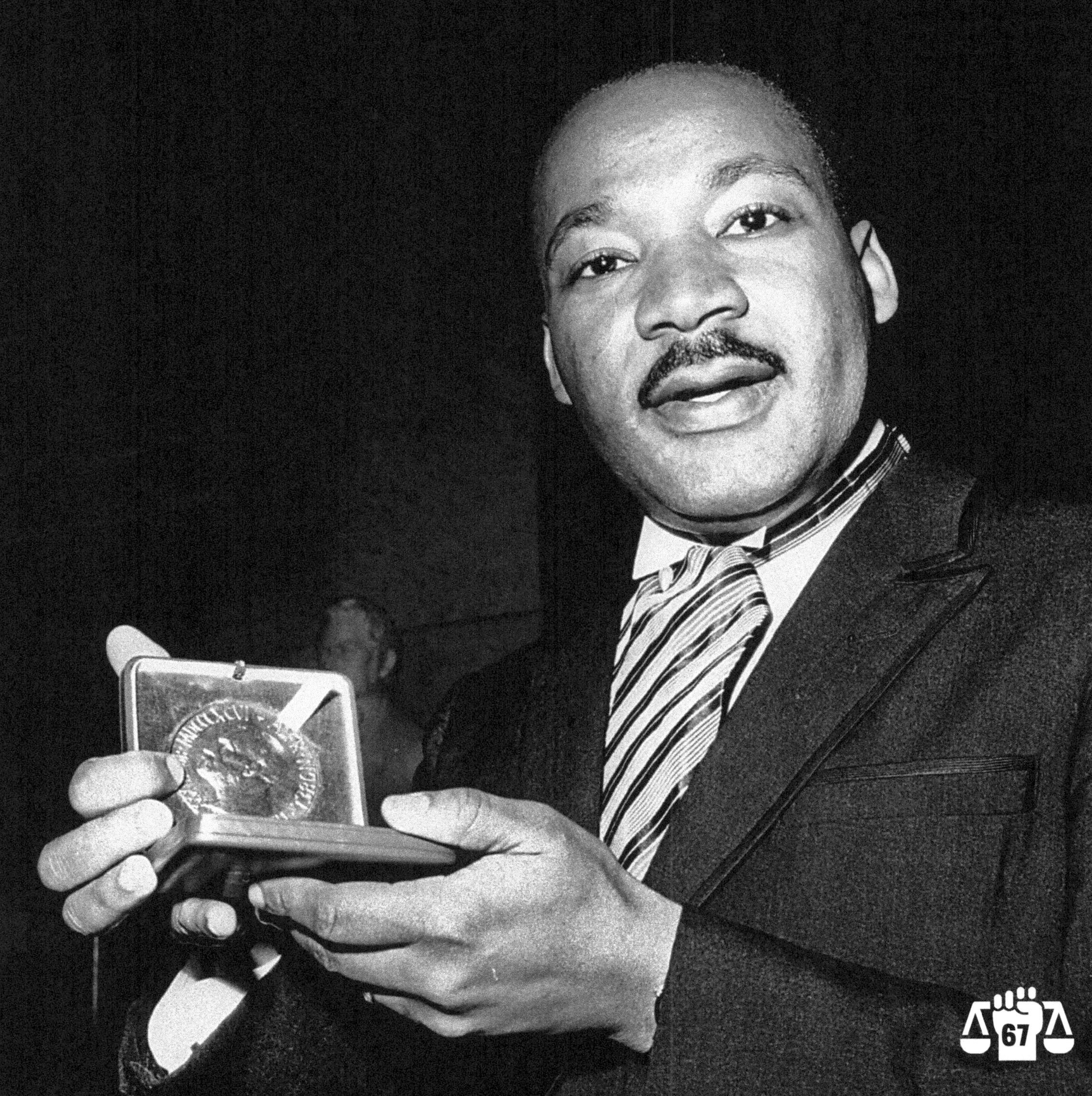

TRUE OR FALSE?

South Africa was governed for over 40 years under a strict system of racial separation called *apartheid*.

THE DIVISIONAL COUNCIL OF THE CAPE
WHITE AREA
BY ORDER SECRETARY
DIE AFDELINGSRAAD VAN DIE KAAP
BLANKE GEBIED
OP LAS SEKRETARIS

TRUE!

The strict separation between whites and nonwhites was used mainly to wield power over the country's nonwhite majority. Apartheid ended in 1991, largely through the work of such activists as Nelson Mandela.

Nelson Mandela casts his vote in South Africa's first election open to all races.

TRUE OR FALSE?

People with disabilities have always enjoyed ready access to public buildings and services.

The Americans with Disabilities Act was passed in 1990 to help improve access to public buildings and services. The act included access for the disabled to government buildings and public transportation.

10:00
TOL 4
F 0
1ST PERIOD
4 TOL
0 F
INDIANA
UCLA
33
INDIANA
10
UCLA
21
13

TRUE OR FALSE?

The law called Title IX was passed primarily to provide increased participation for women in college sports.

FALSE!

Title IX, passed in 1972, protects women from discrimination in every aspect of the educational experience.

TRUE OR FALSE?

Woman suffrage **refers to all the ways women are harmed by discrimination.**

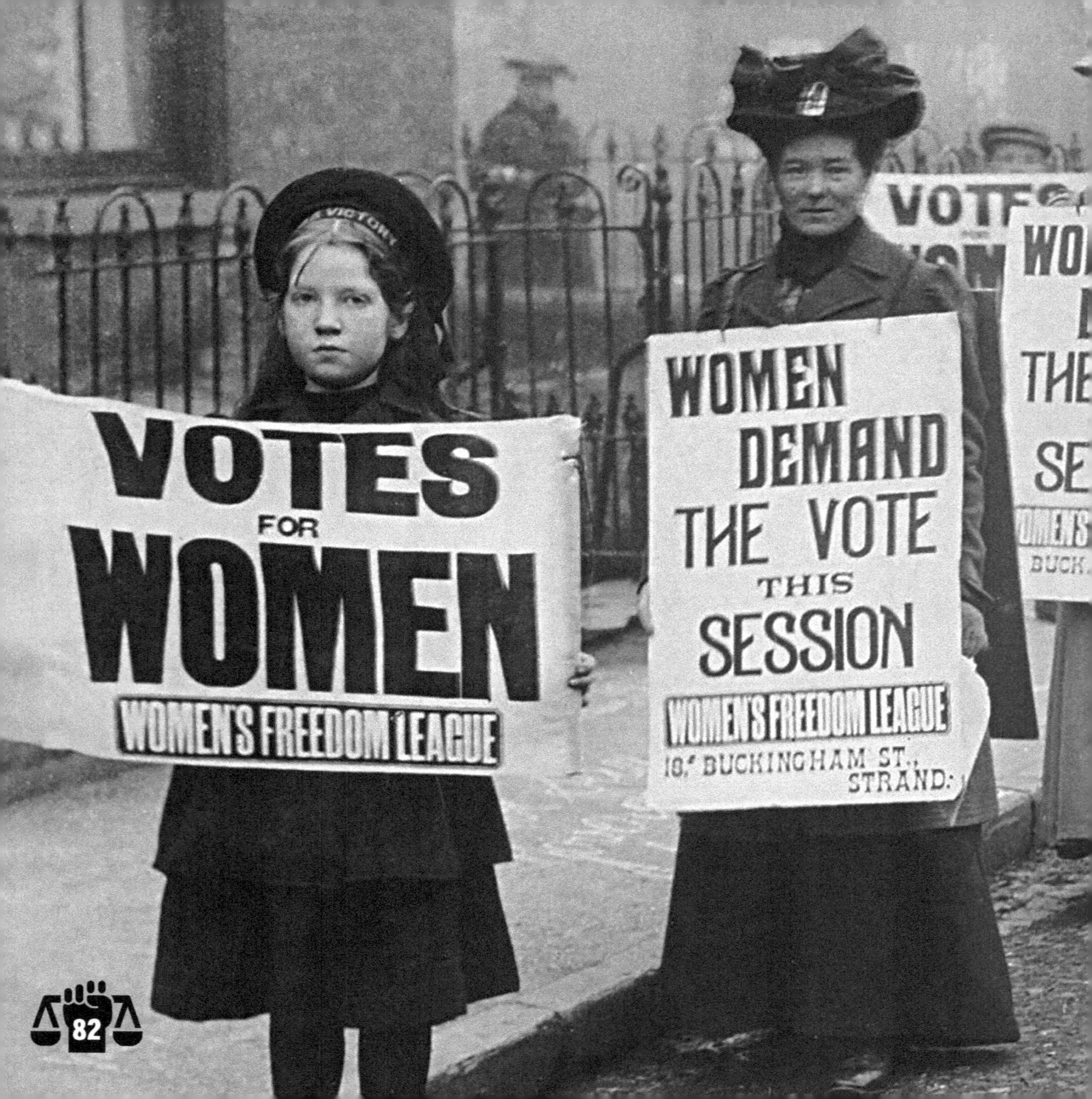
VICTORY
VOTES
FOR
WOMEN
WOMEN'S FREEDOM LEAGUE
WOMEN
DEMAND
THE VOTE
THIS
SESSION
WOMEN'S FREEDOM LEAGUE
18.ª BUCKINGHAM ST.,
STRAND.

Woman suffrage is the right of women to vote. Women in many parts of the world fought for and won the right to vote in the late 1800's.

Women's rights movements in the 1960's brought about many important legal gains for American women.

EQUAL JOBS AND
EDUCATIONAL
OPPORTUNITIES!

President John F. Kennedy signs the Equal Pay Act.

Several laws passed during the 1960's aimed to provide equal rights for women. The Equal Pay Act requires equal pay for men and women doing the same work, and Title VII of the Civil Rights Act prohibits job discrimination for various reasons, including sex.

TRUE OR FALSE?

Unalienable rights **are rights that cannot be extended to creatures from other planets.**

89

Declara

n in the Course of human events, it become

and equal ſtation to which the Laws of N

he ſeparation. —

these are Life, Liberty and the pursui

at whenever any Form of Government

ciples and organizing its powers

d not be changed for light an

the forms to which th

right, it

Unalienable rights are rights that cannot be taken away. Life, liberty, and the pursuit of happiness are mentioned as unalienable rights in the U.S. Declaration of Independence.

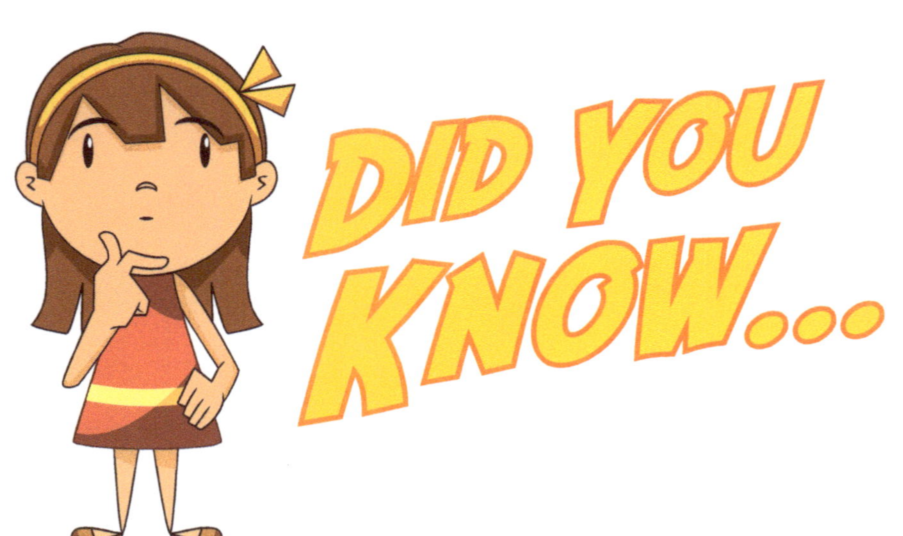

Successful
civil rights protests
of the 1960's included bus boycotts and lunch counter sit-ins.

In writing his famous 1963 "I Have a Dream" speech,
Martin Luther King, Jr.,
drew on his knowledge of the Bible, the Emancipation Proclamation, the Gettysburg Address, and the Declaration of Independence.

The United Nations adopted a Universal **Declaration of Human Rights** in 1948.

People suspected of serious crimes in the United States have the right to **trial by a jury,** a group of ordinary citizens.

Many civil rights activists have been inspired by **Mohandas Gandhi** (1869-1948), who helped free India from British control through nonviolent resistance.

ENGAGE YOUR READER

GUIDED READING PROMPTS

Before Reading

- Allow readers to scan the text and discuss what they notice so far. Highlight the structure of this text and explain that the answers include both evidence and reasoning that support the claim of true or false.
- Explain the literacy skill: *Sometimes authors write a claim and then use evidence and reasoning to help make their point clear. Look for these elements as you read!*

During Reading

- Read each statement and provide time to discuss whether readers believe it to be true or false before turning the page to learn the facts.
- As you read, model how to identify the claims, evidence, and reasoning in the text. Prompt your readers to identify these features as they explore the text, too.
- Encourage readers to further discuss their learning by pausing to discuss surprising information.

After Reading

- Prompt your readers to connect, extend, and challenge their thinking about the text:
  - What will you take away from reading this text?
  - What changes in your thinking happened while reading and learning?
  - What is still challenging your thinking? What questions or wonderings do you still have?

LOOK BACK!

- Prompt readers to look back through the text to identify examples of interesting or thought-provoking claims.
- Challenge readers to explain what makes these examples so engaging.

CURRICULUM CONNECTIONS

These questions and tasks support the following English/Language Arts skills:

- Determining what a text says both explicitly and implicitly
- Citing specific evidence when drawing conclusions
- Interpreting words and phrases used in a text
- Analyzing how the structure of a text affects how it is read.

LITERACY SKILL

Authors make their claims stronger by supporting them with evidence and reasoning.

- A claim is a statement of truth.
- Evidence includes the facts or information that prove whether the claim is true.
- Reasoning includes any logical explanation that describes how the evidence supports the claim.

Examples from the text: Pages 28-31

- Claim: Poll taxes were not charged in order to fund elections.
- Evidence: In 1966, the US Supreme Court ruled poll taxes illegal.
- Reasoning: Many poll taxes were charged to prevent poor people (often formerly enslaved Black people) from voting in U.S. elections.

EXTEND THROUGH WRITING

Challenge readers to create their own True/False questions and answers about civil rights.

- Have readers use a trusted reference, such as www.worldbookonline.com, to research information related to civil rights. Encourage readers to look for key details, fun facts, or surprising features that would make strong True or False statements.
- Give readers one notecard for each claim they research.
- Direct readers to write the claim on the front of the notecard. On the back, readers should describe why that claim is true or false using evidence and reasoning from their research.

MORE WAYS TO ENGAGE!

- Play a game! After considering each claim, have readers signify "true" with a thumb up and "false" with a thumb down. Keep score to see who knows their facts about civil rights the best!
    - Develop collaboration skills by grouping readers together into teams.
- Further discuss any True/False claims that revealed readers' misconceptions. Focus the conversation on *why* they initially thought what they did and how the text helped them learn.

Acknowledgments

Cover © FabrikaSimf/Shutterstock; © WinWin Artlab/Shutterstock; © Hibrida/Shutterstock; © Sylverarts Vectors/Shutterstock

4-22 © Shutterstock
24-25 Library of Congress
26-27 U.S. Department of the Interior
28-29 © bookzv/Shutterstock; UTA Library
30-31 © bookzv/Shutterstock; © Glasshouse Images/Shutterstock
32-33 © photosounds/Shutterstock; © Egor Shilov, Shutterstock
34-35 © photosounds/Shutterstock; Rhododendrites (licensed under CC BY-SA 4.0)
36-37 © f8grapher/Shutterstock
38-39 © RAW-films/Shutterstock; © RWK/AP Photo; © Bob Kreisel, Alamy Images
40-49 © Shutterstock
50-53 Public Domain
54-55 © Cesar Fernandez Dominguez, Shutterstock; © Prostock-studio/Shutterstock
56-57 © Jeff Kinsey, Shutterstock
58-59 Library of Congress
60-61 © ClassicStock/Alamy Images
62-63 United States Department of Justice
64-67 © AP Photo
68-69 © Michele and Tom Grimm, Alamy Images
70-71 © John Parkin, AP Photo
72-75 © Shutterstock
76-77 © SOPA Images Limited/Alamy Images
78-81 © Shutterstock
82-83 Museum of London
84-85 © Science History Images/Alamy Images
86-87 National Archives
88-91 © Shutterstock
92-93 © AP Photo; Public Domain (U.S. Air Force); © D. Kusters/Shutterstock; © Dinodia Photos/Alamy Images; © corgarashu/Shutterstock; © Aleutie/Shutterstock
96 © Willy Sanjuan, Shutterstock

www.ingramcontent.com/pod-product-compliance
Lightning Source LLC
LaVergne TN
LVHW060632110826
845147LV00014B/896

9780716654414